¡Hola!

Communicating With Spanish-Speaking Parents

by Joni Britt

Good
Apple

Editor: *Susan Eddy*

Graphic Design: *Bernadette Hruby*

Cover Illustration: *José Ortega*

Good Apple
A Division of Frank Schaffer Publications, Inc.
23740 Hawthorne Blvd.
Torrance, CA 90505-5927

ISBN 1-56417-898-6

7 8 9 MAL 01

Contents

Introduction

¡Hola! Communicating With Spanish-Speaking Parents provides a quick and reliable solution to some of the problems that may arise when your students' parents speak only Spanish. It is not, however, intended as a total communications system. The book is an important tool, but it should be used whenever possible in addition to contact by bilingual personnel. Personal contact with parents is also an extremely important part of an effective school-home communications system.

This handbook has been formatted so that it can be easily used by school personnel with limited or no knowledge of the Spanish language. The majority of the letters use a check system for choosing the desired message. Teachers use Spanish only when adding dates to the forms. A list of the Spanish days of the week and months of the year can be found on page 5. The English version of each letter precedes the Spanish version. Very short communications are printed two to a page.

Many Spanish-speaking parents have some English language skills. If you are unsure of the extent of these skills, consider photocopying the Spanish version on one side of the letter and English on the reverse. Parents may wish to use the English version of the school supplies letter to communicate with store employees when purchasing supplies.

The disk that is enclosed with this book is IBM-compatible but can be read by Macintosh as well. Minimum Macintosh requirements: System 7.1, Macintosh IIs and up. Use of the disk enables you to type in appropriate names, dates, phone numbers, and so on, as well as to customize the letters in any way you like.

Spanish Days and Months

Use the following information when dating your communications with Spanish-speaking parents. Days of the week and months of the year are *not* capitalized in Spanish. When writing the date, the day usually precedes the month. Example: 12 de mayo de 1999.

Months of the Year

January	enero
February	febrero
March	marzo
April	abril
May	mayo
June	junio
July	julio
August	agosto
September	septiembre
October	octubre
November	noviembre
December	diciembre

Days of the Week

Sunday	domingo
Monday	lunes
Tuesday	martes
Wednesday	miércoles
Thursday	jueves
Friday	viernes
Saturday	sábado

_____

Dear Family:

I am happy that _____ will be a part of my classroom this
                           (child's name)

year. I'm looking forward to a good year. I would like to answer some of the
questions you may have.

Classroom Organization

In the elementary classroom, one teacher usually teaches all the daily
subjects, such as reading, writing, mathematics, spelling, English, social
studies, science, and health. Physical education, art, music and library skills
are usually taught by a special teacher. If your child's classroom is not
being conducted in this manner, you will be informed by the teacher, and the
new procedure will be explained.

Grades

Most classrooms use a district-wide grading system for report cards and
conferences. This is usually based on either a letter or a number system.
Our class uses the following:

_____ A, B, C, D, F (A = superior, F = failing)

_____ 1, 2, 3, 4, 5 (1 = superior, 5 = failing)

_____ _____

_____

Your child's ability and skill levels are taken into consideration in the grading
process. These levels are noted on the report cards, which are sent out four
times a year.

Every classroom should be a pleasant place to learn. To help accomplish
this, each class has a discipline plan. The plan for our class will be sent
home the first week of school. Please contact me if you do not understand
any part of the plan or if you have any other questions.

I look forward to meeting you personally in the near future. I hope you will
plan to come to as many school activities as possible. Feel free to contact

me at _____ if you wish to visit our class or help
              (phone number)
in the classroom.

_____   _____
(teacher's signature)   (room number)

Estimada familia:

Me alegro de que _____ esté en mi clase este año. Espero
(nombre del estudiante)

tener un buen año. Me gustaría contestar algunas preguntas que Uds.
puedan tener.

La organización de la clase

En la escuela primaria, generalmente, hay un maestro para cada clase.
Este maestro enseña las materias de Lectura, Escritura, Matemáticas,
Inglés, Estudios sociales, Ciencias, Salud y Arte. Otro maestro enseña las
materias de Educación física, Música, y Biblioteca.

Si la clase de su hijo o hija no está organizada de esta forma, el maestro
les explicará la organización.

Las calificaciones

El districto escolar establece el sistema de calificar para todas las
escuelas. Se usa este sistema para los informes de calificación. Se usan
letras o números para las calificaciones. Nuestra clase usa lo siguiente:

_____ A, B, C, D, F (A= Sobresaliente, F = Desaprobado)

_____ 1, 2, 3, 4, 5 (1 = Sobresaliente, 5 = Desaprobado)

_____ _____

_____

Para calificar, se considera el nivel de habilidad del estudiante. Estos
niveles estarán escritos en el informe de calificación, que se envía a la
casa cuatro veces al año.

Las reglas de disciplina en la clase

Cada clase debe ser un lugar agradable para aprender. Para lograr este
objetivo, cada clase tiene sus reglas de disciplina. Les enviaré las reglas
durante la primera semana de clase. Si Uds. no las entienden o tienen
otras preguntas, les agradecería que me llamaran.

Espero conocerlos personalmente pronto. Si les es posible, vengan a las
actividades de la escuela frecuentemente. Si quieren visitar la clase o ayudar en la misma, les agradecería que me lo dejaran saber.

_____   _____

(Firma del Maestro/a)   (Número del salón)

How Parents Can Help at Home

Parents are an important part of a child's education. Research shows that parental interest and involvement in school has a positive effect on a child's academic progress. We will try to keep you informed about your child's progress and the activities at school. Letters and forms written in Spanish and a bilingual contact person are available to help in our communication.

Here are some ways to help your child be a successful student.

1. Take an interest in your child's work by looking at his or her papers. Praise work that is well done.

2. Establish a regular time and place for your child to do homework. Each child should develop the habit of studying at home.

3. Practice the weekly spelling words with your child. This is the schedule for spelling in my class:

   Word lists come home on _____.

   Tests are given on _____.

4. Encourage your child to read every day at home. When appropriate, read aloud to your child. In some cases, books will be assigned or book reports will be required. Reading is an important skill for all academic work.

5. Basic mathematical skills need to be reviewed regularly, both at school and at home. Special homework will be assigned periodically. Please go over this work with your child.

Parent involvement at home is so helpful. Your child will love knowing that you are interested in his or her schoolwork and activities.

Cómo los padres pueden ayudar en la casa

Ustedes, como padres, constituyen una parte importante en la educación de su hijo o hija. Estudios educacionales nos dicen que el interés y la participación de los padres tienen un efecto positivo en el progreso académico de los hijos. Nosotros trataremos de informarles del progreso de su hijo o hija, y también, de las actividades de la escuela. Cartas en español, y la ayuda de una persona bilingüe nos facilitarán la comunicación con Uds.

Aquí les ofrecemos unas sugerencias para ayudar a que su hijo o hija sea un estudiante destacado:

1. Tomen interés en el trabajo de su hijo o hija. Revisen la tarea, y felicítenle por un trabajo bien hecho. Si su hijo o hija tiene problemas con cierta tarea, revísela y corríjala.

2. Cada estudiante debe de estudiar en la casa. Es importante fijar una hora y lugar para hacer las tareas.

3. Cada semana se enseñan nuevas palabras del vocabulario. Es importante estudiar estas palabras con su hijo o hija. El horario de ortografía para mi clase es:

   Las listas de palabras irán a casa los _____.

   El examen será el _____.

4. Su hijo o hija debe de leer cada noche en la casa. También, Uds. podrían leerle en voz alta a su hijo o hija. Algunas veces, su hijo o hija tendrá un libro especial para leer, o hacer un reporte acerca del libro. El saber leer es muy importante para las otras materias de la escuela.

5. Es importante estudiar las lecciones de matemáticas regularmente. Su ayuda es necesaria para repasar las lecciones. Cada día su hijo o hija tendrá trabajo, y de vez en cuando una tarea especial. Les agradecería que revisaran este trabajo junto con su hijo o hija.

La ayuda de los padres en la casa es esencial. Su hijo o hija necesita saber que Uds. están interesados en el trabajo y las actividades que hace en la escuela.

_____

Hello _____!
(child's name)

Welcome to _____ grade! To help you prepare for school, I have included a list of materials you will need for my class. Please label the items with your name and bring them with you the first day of school. **Only the items marked with an X are needed.**

_____ 1 box 16 or 24 crayons

_____ #2 pencils*

_____ 1 box colored pencils

_____ 1 eraser

_____ ballpoint pens (_____red _____blue _____black)*

_____ felt-tipped markers*

_____ 1 package wide-rule paper

_____ 3-ring binder

_____ 1 pair scissors

_____ glue stick(s)*

_____ 1 box facial tissues

_____ 1 backpack or bookbag

I hope you had a nice summer. See you soon!

_____

signature

* Add number of items you wish the child to bring.

_____

Hola, _____
      (Nombre del estudiante)

¡Bienvenido/a al _____ grado! Para ayudarte con las preparaciones para la escuela, aquí te incluyo una lista de cosas que necesitas para mi clase. Te agradezco que escribas tu nombre en cada cosa y la traigas el primer día de clases. **Sólo necesitas las cosas que tengan una X delante del nombre.**

_____1 Caja de 16 o 24 creyones

_____ Lápices de escribir No. 2*

_____1 Caja de lápices de colores

_____1 Goma de borrar

_____*Bolígrafos (_____ rojo _____ azul _____ negro)

_____1 Caja de marcadores de punta de fieltro

_____1 Paquete de papel (tamaño "Wide Ruler)

_____1 Carpeta de tres anillos (de 1 1/2 pulgadas de ancho)

_____1 Par de tijeras

_____*Barras de pegamento

_____1 Caja de toallitas faciales

_____1 Mochila o bolsa para los libros

Espero que te hayas divertido durante el verano. Nos vemos pronto.

_____

(Firma del maestro/a)

* Maestro/a: Anote la cantidad que desea que el estudiante
   traiga a la clase.

_____

Dear Family:

My name is _____. I am _____ teacher.
　　　　　　　(teacher's name)　　　　　　　　　(child's name)

I do not speak Spanish, but if you have any questions or concerns, you may contact

_____ at _____ .
　　　　　　　(bilingual contact)　　　　　　　　　　　　(phone number)

Please keep this name and telephone number handy for use during the year. Also feel free to write notes to me in Spanish. I will have them translated here at school.

_____

(teacher's signature)

_____

Estimada familia:

Me llamo _____ .

Soy el maestro/la maestra de _____.
　　　　　　　　　　　　　　　(Nombre del estudiante)

Yo no hablo español, pero Uds. pueden comunicarse con _____

_____ en el número _____ si tienen preguntas.
　(Persona bilingüe)　　　　　　　　(Número de teléfono)

Les agradecería que conservaran este nombre y número de teléfono durante todo el año escolar. Si lo desean, también me pueden escribir cartas en español, y alguien me las traducirá aquí en la escuela. Gracias.

_____

(Firma del maestro/a)

_____

Dear Family:

Please complete the following forms and return them to school with your child as soon as possible. If you have any questions you may contact

_____ at _____ .
(bilingual contact)   (phone number)

Thank you for your help.

_____
(teacher's signature)

_____

Estimada familia:

Les agradecería que completaran los formularios siguientes y los devolvieran con su hijo o hija a la escuela lo más pronto posible.

Si Uds. tienen preguntas pueden llamar a

_____ al número _____ .
(Persona bilingüe)   (Número de teléfono)

Gracias por su ayuda.

_____

(Firma del maestro/a)

_____

Dear Family:

Our normal school day is Monday through Friday from _____ a.m. to

_____ p.m. Your child should arrive no earlier than _____ a.m. and should leave immediately upon dismissal in the afternoon.

Please contact the school if you have any questions.
Thank you.

_____

(teacher's signature)

_____

Estimada familia:

El horario normal de la escuela es de lunes a viernes, desde las _____

de la mañana, hasta las _____ de la tarde. Su hijo o hija no debe de

llegar antes de las _____ de la mañana, y debe retirarse de la escuela inmediatemente después de concluir las clases en la tarde.
Les agradeceríamos que llamaran a la escuela si tienen preguntas.
Gracias,

_____

(Firma del maestro/a)

_____

Dear Family:

There will be no school on _____.
(date)

School will resume at the regular hour on _____.
(date)

_____
(teacher's signature)

_____

Estimada familia:

No habrá clases el día_____.
(Fecha)

El día_____, la escuela reanudará su horario habitual.
(Fecha)

_____
(Firma del maestro/a)

_____

Dear Family:

There will be an early dismissal on _____.
(date)

School will be dismissed at _____.

School lunch _____ will be served.

_____ will not be served.

School will resume at the regular hour on _____.
(date)

_____
(teacher's signature)

_____

Estimada familia:

El día _____ las clases terminarán antes del horario habitual.
(Fecha)

Los estudiantes saldrán a las _____ en punto.

_____ SÍ se servirá almuerzo en la escuela.

_____ NO se servirá almuerzo en la escuela.

La escuela reanudará las clases en su horario habitual el día _____.
(Fecha)

_____
(Firma del maestro/a)

_____

Dear Family:

_____ was absent on _____.
    (child's name)   (date)

Please give the reason for absence and send it to school with your child.

Thank you.

_____ Illness

_____ Visit to the doctor or dentist

_____ Other (Please explain below)

_____

_____

_____

_____
(teacher's signature)

_____
(parent's signature)

_____

Estimada familia:

_____ faltó a clases el día _____.
   (Nombre del estudiante)   (Fecha)

Les agradecería que me informaran el motivo de la ausencia, firmaran esta carta y la devolvieran a la escuela con su hijo o hija.

_____ Enfermedad

_____ Cita con el doctor o el dentista

_____ Otra causa (expliquen abajo)

_____

_____

_____

_____
(Firma del maestro/a)

_____
(Firma de los padres)

_____

Dear Family:

Frequent absences are affecting _____'s progress in school.
(child's name)

Please encourage completion of the work _____ has missed.
Thank you.

_____ See attached assignment(s).

_____ See assignment sheet.

_____
(teacher's signature)

- -
(Cut here and return to school.)

I understand that _____ needs to complete work.
(child's name)

_____ I will encourage completion of the work.

_____ I would like to discuss this matter.

_____
(parent's signature)

_____
(telephone number)

_____

Estimada familia:

Las frecuentes ausencias de _____

(Nombre del estudiante)

afectan su adelanto en la escuela. Animen a su hijo o hija a que se ponga al día en las clases que ha perdido y a que realice las tareas asignadas.

_____ Vean Uds. la tarea adjunta.

_____ Vean Uds. la hoja de tarea.

_____

(Firma del maestro/a)

- -

(Corten aquí y devuelvan esta parte a la escuela.)

Entiendo que _____ necesita ponerse al

(Nombre del estudiante)

día en las tareas que perdió por ausencias.

_____ Animaré a mi hijo o hija a realizar la tarea.

_____ Me gustaría hablar con Ud. sobre este asunto.

_____

(Firma de los padres)

_____

(Número de teléfono)

_____

Dear Family:

I have scheduled an appointment for a conference concerning

_____'s progress in school

(child's name)

at _____ on _____ in room _____.

(time)   (date)

Please respond below and return the form to school. I'm looking forward to meeting with you. Thank you.

_____

(teacher's signature)

- -

(Cut here and return to school.)

_____ Yes, I/we can come to the conference.

_____ No, I/we can't come at that time.

_____ is better.

_____

(parent's signature)

_____

(telephone number)

_____

Estimados Sr. y Sra. _____,
                              (Nombre de los padres)

He programado una reunión con Uds. para hablar del desarrollo de

_____ en la escuela.
 (Nombre del estudiante)

La reunión es a las _____, el día_____,

en el salón número _____.

Les agradecería que me contestaran con el talón de abajo y lo
devolvieran a la escuela.

Espero verlos en la reunión.

_____

(Firma del maestro/a)

- -

(Corten aquí y devuelvan esta parte a la escuela.)

_____ Sí, podemos asistir a la reunión en esa fecha.

_____ No, no podemos asistir en esa fecha.

El día _____ sería mejor para nosotros.

_____

(Firma de los padres)

_____

(Número de teléfono)

_____

Dear _____ **Family:**

This notice is to remind you of the conference concerning

_____ at _____ on _____ in room _____.
(child's name)   (time)   (date)

I look forward to seeing you then!

_____
(teacher's signature)

_____

Estimados Sr. y Sra. _____,
                    (Nombre de los padres)

Esta nota es para recordarles de la reunión acerca de _____
                                          (Nombre del estudiante)

a las _____ , el día _____, en el salón número _____.
Espero verlos en la reunión.

_____
(Firma del maestro/a)

_____

Dear Family:

_____ is currently in danger of
　　　(child's name)

receiving a poor grade in _____ class.
　　　　　　　　　　　　　　　(subject)

Grade: _____ as of _____.
　　　　　　　　　(date)

Reasons for lack of progress:

_____ Absences are affecting school work.

_____ Books or materials are not brought to class.

_____ Assignments are not completed regularly.

_____ Class participation is poor.

_____ Study habits need improving.

Your assistance in this matter will be appreciated. Thank you.

_____
(teacher's signature)

- -

(Cut here and return to school.)

_____ I have read this and understand the problem.

_____ I wish to meet with you about this problem.

_____ _____

_____

_____

_____ _____ _____
(child's name) 　　　(parent's signature) 　　(date)

_____

Estimada familia:

_____ de la clase de _____
(Nombre del estudiante)   (Asignatura)

está en peligro de desaprobar la asignatura.

Nota: _____ Hasta el día _____.
                              (Fecha)

La causa(s) de falta de progreso es:

_____ El estudiante no está trabajando al nivel de sus habilidades.

_____ Las ausencias afectan su trabajo.

_____ No lleva los libros o materiales escolares a la clase.

_____ No hace la tarea con regularidad.

_____ Casi no participa en clase.

_____ Necesita mejorar su modo de estudiar.

Les agradecería su ayuda en este asunto. Gracias.

_____
(Firma del maestro/a)

- -

(Corten aquí y devuelvan esta parte a la escuela.)

Les agradecería que firmaran esta parte de la nota y la devolvieran a la escuela con su hijo o hija en el siguiente día escolar.

_____ Hemos leído este aviso y entendemos el problema.

_____ Queremos tener una reunión con Ud. sobre este problema.

_____ _____

_____

_____

_____ _____ _____
(Nombre del estudiante)   (Firma de los padres)   (Fecha)

_____

Dear Family:

Below is a progress report for _____ as of _____ .
(child's name)   (date)

___Mathematics _____ .

___Reading _____ .

___Penmanship _____ .

___Spelling _____ .

___English _____ .

___Social Studies _____ .

___Science _____ .

___Health _____ .

Please contact me if you have any questions.

_____
(teacher's signature)

- -

(Cut here and return to school.)

I have seen the progress report for _____ .
(child's name)

_____ I would like to schedule a conference.

_____
(parent's signature)

_____
(telephone number)

26

_____

Estimada familia:

Abajo tienen un informe del progreso de _____
(Nombre del estudiante)

hasta el día _____.
(Fecha)

____ Matemáticas_____.

____ Lectura_____.

____ Caligrafía_____.

____ Ortografía_____.

____ Inglés_____.

____ Estudios sociales_____.

____ Ciencias_____.

____ Salud_____.

Les agradecería que me llamaran si tienen preguntas.

_____

(Firma del maestro/a)

- -

(Corten aquí y devuelvan esta parte a la escuela.)

Hemos visto el informe de progreso de _____.
(Nombre del estudiante)

_____

(Firma de los padres)

_____

(Número de teléfono)

STUDENT GRADE REPORT

SCHOOL _____

City _____ State _____

Student Name _____

Grade _____ Year _____

Teacher _____

Principal _____

Academic Skills

	Quarter			
	1	2	3	4
Reading ....Skills				
Effort				
Penmanship .....Skills				
Effort				
English ....Skills				
Effort				
Spelling ....Skills				
Effort				
Mathematics ....Skills				
Effort				
Health ....Skills				
Effort				
Science ....Skills				
Effort				
Social Studies ...Skills				
Effort				
Library ....Skills				
Effort				
Music ....Skills				
Effort				
P.E. ....Skills				
Effort				
Art ....Skills				
Effort				

Attendance

	Quarter			
	1	2	3	4
Days Present				
Days Absent				
Days Tardy				

Study Skills

Follows directions				
Completes work on time ..				
Is neat				
Listens to instructions ..				
Uses extra time wisely ...				
Works independently				

Social Skills

Works well with others ...				
Shows respect to adults .				
Follows school rules				
Shows self control				

Grading System

1 or **A** - Outstanding
2 or **B** - Above Average
3 or **C** - Average-Satisfactory
4 or **D** - Below Average
5 or **F** - Failed Minimum level
N - No Grade at this time
* - Below grade level or
Special Class

EFFORT:
O - Outstanding
S - Satisfactory
U - Unsatisfactory

Grade Assignment Next Year: _____

Teacher Next Year: _____

Teacher's Signature _____

INFORME DE CALIFICACIONES FINALES DEL ESTUDIANTE

Escuela _____

Ciudad _____ Estado _____

Nombre del estudiante _____

Grado _____ Año _____

Maestro/a _____

Director _____

Aptitudes académicas

	Trimestre			
	1	2	3	4
Lectura . . . . .Aptitud				
Esfuerzo				
Caligrafía . . . . . . .Aptitud				
Esfuerzo				
Inglés . . . . .Aptitud				
Esfuerzo				
Ortografía . . . . . .Aptitud				
Esfuerzo				
Matemáticas . . . . .Aptitud				
Esfuerzo				
Salud . . . . .Aptitud				
Esfuerzo				
Ciencias . . . . .Aptitud				
Esfuerzo				
Estudios sociales . . .Aptitud				
Esfuerzo				
Biblioteca . . . . . . .Aptitud				
Esfuerzo				
Música . . . . .Aptitud				
Esfuerzo				
Educación física. . .Esfuerzo				
Esfuerzo				
Arte . . . . .Aptitud				
Esfuerzo				

Asistencia

	Trimestre			
	1	2	3	4
Días presente				
Días ausente				
Tardanzas				

Aptitudes para el estudio

Sigue instrucciones				
Termina el trabajo a tiempo .				
Es Ordenado/s				
Escucha las instrucciones . .				
Hace buen uso del tiempo libre .				
Trabaja independientemente .				

Aptitudes sociales

Trabaja bien con otros				
Respeta a los adultos				
Sigue las reglas de la escuela				
Demuestra control				

Sistema de calificaciones

1 o A - Sobresaliente
2 o B - Muy bien
3 o C - Muy bien-Satisfactorio
4 o D - Bajo promedio
5 o F - Desaprobado
N - No hay calificación ahora
* - Debajo del nivel del grado o Clase especial

Esfuerzo
O - Sobresaliente
S - Satisfactorio
U - No Satisfactorio

Debe asistir al _____ grado el próximo año.

Maestro/a para el próximo año: _____

Firma del maestro/a: _____

29

_____

Dear Family:

_____ has not turned in assigned work in the following areas:
(child's name)

____Mathematics _____

____Reading _____

____Penmanship _____

____Spelling _____

____English _____

____Social Studies _____

____Science _____

____Health _____

____Other (see attached)

Please encourage your child to complete this work. Thank you.

_____
(teacher's signature)

- -

(Cut here and return to school.)

I am aware that _____ has not completed work.
(child's name)

_____
(parent's signature)

_____

Estimada familia:

_____ no ha entregado las tareas en las siguientes asignaturas:
(Nombre del estudiante)

___ Matemáticas_____.

___ Lectura_____.

___ Caligrafía_____.

___ Ortografía_____.

___ Inglés_____.

___ Estudios sociales_____.

___ Ciencias_____.

___ Salud_____.

___ Otro: Vean las hojas adjuntas.

Les agradecería que animaran a su hijo o hija a terminar sus tareas.

_____

(Firma del maestro/a)

- -

(Corten aquí y devuelvan esta parte a la escuela.)

Estamos enterados de que_____no ha terminado sus tareas.
(Nombre del estudiante)

_____

(Firma de los padres)

_____

Dear Family:

_____ tried his or her best today to complete the attached work but is having difficulty. Could you help _____ complete this work tonight as homework, then sign and return it to school tomorrow?

Thank you for your help and support in this area of your child's education.

_____
(teacher's signature)

_____
(school telephone number)

_____
(parent's signature)

_____

Estimada familia:

Su hijo o hija puso todo su empeño para hacer el trabajo que aquí les adjunto, pero tuvo dificultades en terminarlo. ¿Le podrían ayudar a terminar el trabajo esta noche, firmarlo y devolverlo a la escuela mañana?

Les agradezco su ayuda y apoyo en esta área de la educación de su hijo o hija.

_____
(Firma del maestro/a)

_____
(Número de teléfono de la escuela)

_____
(Firma de los padres)

_____

Dear Family:

_____ chose not to use his/her time wisely today during class. The attached work will need to be completed tonight as homework. This sheet should be signed and returned to school tomorrow.

Thank you for your help and support in this area of your child's education.

_____
(teacher's signature)

_____
(school telephone number)

_____
(parent's signature)

_____

Estimada familia:

Su hijo o hija decidió no usar su tiempo provechosamente hoy en clases. Él o ella debe terminar el trabajo adjunto esta noche como tarea. Les agradezco que firmen esta carta y la devuelvan a la escuela mañana con su hijo o hija.

Les agradezco su cooperación en esta área de la educación de su hijo o hija.

_____
(Firma del maestro/a)

_____
(Número de teléfono de la escuela)

_____
(Firma de los padres)

_____

Dear Family:

Our class is studying the following math topics:

_____ Recognizing numbers from 1 to 20

_____ Counting from 1 to 20

_____ Counting by 5s (5, 10, 15, 20)

_____ Writing numbers correctly

_____ Recognizing basic shapes

_____ Time

_____ Identifying coins (penny, nickel, dime)

_____ Identifying patterns

Attached is a sheet that will give you an example of the work we are doing. Please encourage your child to study these skills at home.

Thank you for your help.

_____

(teacher's signature)

_____

Estimada familia:

En nuestra clase de matemáticas estamos estudiando los siguientes temas:

_____ Reconocer los números del 1 al 20

_____ Contar del 1 al 20

_____ Contar de 5 en 5 (5, 10, 15, 20)

_____ Escribir los números correctamente

_____ Reconocer las figuras básicas

_____ Leer la hora

_____ Identificar monedas de 1, 5, 10, 25 centavos

_____ Identificar patrones

Aquí les adjunto un ejemplo de lo que estamos estudiando. Les agradezco que animen a su hijo o hija a estudiar estas destrezas en la casa.

Gracias por su ayuda.

_____

(Firma del maestro/a)

_____

Dear Family:

Our class is studying the following math topics:

_____ Addition facts from 1 to 10   _____ Time

_____ Subtraction facts from 1 to 10   _____ Geometric shapes

_____ Adding 2- and 3-digit numbers   _____ Measurement

_____ Subtracting 2- and 3-digit numbers   _____ Place value

_____ Basic multiplication facts   _____ Money

Attached is a sheet that will give you an example of the work we are doing. Please encourage your child to study these skills at home.

Thank you for your help.

_____

(teacher's signature)

_____

Estimada familia:

En nuestra clase de matemáticas estamos estudiando los siguientes temas:

_____ Suma de números del 1 al 10   _____ Leer la hora

_____ Resta de números del 1 al 10   _____ Figuras geométricas

_____ Suma de números de 2 y 3 dígitos   _____ Medidas

_____ Resta de números de 2 y 3 dígitos   _____ Decimales

_____ Tabla de multiplicar (multiplicación)   _____ Dinero

Aquí les adjunto un ejemplo de lo que estamos estudiando. Les agradezco que animen a su hijo o hija a estudiar estas destrezas en la casa.

Gracias por su ayuda.

_____

(Firma del maestro/a)

_____

Dear Family:

Our class is studying the following math topics:

_____ Addition of numbers with 3 or more digits   _____ Fractions

_____ Subtraction of numbers with 3 or more digits   _____ Geometry

_____ Basic multiplication facts   _____ Measurement

_____ Basic division facts

_____ Multiplication of numbers with 2 or more digits

_____ Division of numbers with 2 or more digits

Attached is a sheet that will give you an example of the work we are doing. Please encourage your child to study these skills at home.

Thank you for your help!

_____

(teacher's signature)

_____

Estimada familia:

En nuestra clase de matemáticas estamos estudiando los siguientes temas:

_____ Suma de números con 3 o más dígitos   _____ Fracciones

_____ Resta de números con 3 o más dígitos   _____ Geometría

_____ Tabla de multiplicar (multiplicación)   _____ Medidas

_____ Tabla de dividir (división)

_____ Multiplicación de números con 2 o más dígitos

_____ División de números con 2 o más dígitos

Aquí les adjunto un ejemplo de lo que estamos estudiando. Les agradezco que animen a su hijo o hija a estudiar estas destrezas en la casa.

Gracias por su ayuda.

_____

(Firma del maestro/a)

_____

Dear Family:

I am proud of_____'s efforts in school.
                    (child's name)

_____ Has a positive attitude

_____ Completes work on time

_____ Strives to do his or her best

_____ Is helpful to others

_____ Respects self, peers, and adults

_____ Has shown improved behavior

_____ Has shown improvement in work

You and your child should be proud, too!

_____
(teacher's signature)

_____

Estimada familia:

¡Estoy muy orgulloso/a del esfuerzo de

_____ en la escuela!
           (Nombre del estudiante)

_____ Tiene una actitud muy positiva.

_____ Termina el trabajo a tiempo.

_____ Trata de hacer su mejor trabajo.

_____ Ayuda a los demás.

_____ Se respeta a sí mismo/a, a sus compañeros y
         a los adultos.

_____ Su comportamiento ha mejorado.

_____ Su trabajo ha mejorado.

¡Su hijo/hija debe de estar orgulloso/a de su esfuerzo!

_____
(Firma del maestro/a)

_____

Dear Family:

I am proud of _____'s efforts in math.
(child's name)

_____ Completes work on time

_____ Uses good thinking skills

_____ Has learned a basic skill

_____ Works independently

_____ Listens effectively

_____ Works neatly

_____ Grades show improvement

_____ Test scores are high

You and your child should be proud, too!

_____
(teacher's signature)

_____

Estimada familia:

Estoy muy orgulloso/a del esfuerzo de

_____ en las matemáticas.
(Nombre del estudiante)

_____ Termina el trabajo a tiempo.

_____ Piensa con cuidado.

_____ Ha aprendido la lección.

_____ Trabaja independientemente.

_____ Escucha bien.

_____ Trabaja con cuidado.

_____ Ha mejorado su nota.

_____ Tuvo una nota alta en el último examen.

¡Su hijo o hija debe sentirse muy orgulloso/a de sus logros!

_____
(Firma del maestro/a)

_____

Dear Family:

I am proud of _____'s efforts in reading.
       (child's name)

_____ Reads well orally

_____ Understands what he or she reads

_____ Has improved reading skills

_____ Uses good thinking skills

_____ Works independently

_____ Reads more at home

_____ Grade shows improvement

_____ Completes work on time

You and your child should be proud, too!

_____
(teacher's signature)

_____

Estimada familia:

¡Estoy muy orgulloso/a del esfuerzo de

_____ en lectura!
    (Nombre del estudiante)

_____ Lee bien en voz alta.

_____ Entiende lo que lee.

_____ Ha mejorado su destreza en la lectura.

_____ Tiene buenas destrezas analíticas.

_____ Trabaja independientemente.

_____ Lee más en la casa.

_____ Ha mejorado sus calificaciones.

_____ Termina los trabajos a tiempo.

¡Su hijo o hija se debe sentir muy orgulloso/a de su progreso!

_____

(Firma del maestro/a)

_____

Dear Family:

I am proud of _____'s efforts in my class.
(child's name)

_____ Completed an important project

_____ Improved his or her skills

_____ Observes class rules

_____ Listens effectively

_____ Works independently

_____ Completes work on time

_____ Is pleasant and cooperative

You and your child should be proud of his or her work in

_____ music

_____ physical education

_____ library

_____ art

_____ computers

_____
(teacher's signature)

_____

Estimada familia:

¡Estoy muy orgulloso/a del esfuerzo de

_____ en mi clase!
    (Nombre del estudiante)

_____ Terminó un proyecto importante.

_____ Mejoró su aptitud.

_____ Obedece las reglas de la clase.

_____ Escucha bien.

_____ Trabaja independientemente.

_____ Termina el trabajo a tiempo.

_____ Es agradable y cooperador/a.

Su hijo o hija debe sentirse orgulloso/a de su trabajo en:

_____ Música

_____ Educación física

_____ Biblioteca

_____ Arte

_____ Computadora

_____

(Firma del maestro/a)

_____

Dear Family:

_____ has been misbehaving at school.
      (child's name)

After speaking with him or her, the following behavior still continues.

_____ Is disrespectful to school adults

_____ Is disrespectful to peers

_____ Has disrespect for school property

_____ Fights

_____ Uses bad language

_____ Frequently breaks playground rules

_____ Frequently breaks classroom rules

Please help me in encouraging an improvement in behavior. Thank you.

_____

(teacher's signature)

_____ Please call for a conference.

- -

(Cut here and return to school.)

I understand that _____ is misbehaving,
                    (child's name)

and I will help encourage a change.

_____

(parent's signature)

_____

Estimada familia:

_____ no se comporta bien en la escuela.
 (Nombre del estudiante)

Después de hablar con él/ella, su mala conducta continuó
de la siguiente forma:

_____ No respeta a los adultos de la escuela.

_____ No respeta a los compañeros.

_____ No respeta la propiedad de la escuela.

_____ Pelea.

_____ Dice malas palabras.

_____ Desobedece las reglas del recreo continuamente.

_____ Desobedece las reglas de la clase continuamente.

**Les agradecería su cooperación para lograr que su hijo o hija
mejore su conducta. Gracias.**

_____
(Firma del maestro/a)

_____ Favor de llamarme para reunirnos.

- -

(Corten aquí y devuelvan esta parte a la escuela)

Estamos enterados de que _____ se está
                     (Nombre del estudiante)

portando mal, y ayudaremos a que cambie favorablemente su conducta.

_____
(Firma de los padres)

_____

Dear Family:

_____ has misbehaved several times at school
(child's name)

_____ today

_____ this week

_____ this quarter

Therefore,

_____ he/she served detention during school today.

_____ he/she must serve detention after school

on _____ from _____ to _____.
(date)   (time)

**Please talk to your child so that this problem will not happen again.
Thank you.**

_____
(teacher's signature)

- -

(Cut here and return to school.)

Detention

Please sign and return on the next school day.

_____ We have read this notice.

_____ We wish to have a meeting with you about this problem.

_____
(student's signature)

_____
(parent's signature)

_____
(telephone number)

_____

Estimada familia:

_____ se ha portado mal varias veces en la escuela
(Nombre del estudiante)

_____ hoy,

_____ esta semana,

_____ este trimestre.

Por este motivo,

_____ el/ella cumplió una penitencia durante las clases hoy.

_____ el/ella debe cumplir una penitencia después de las clases,

el día _____ de _____ a _____.
(Fecha)   (Horario)

Les agradecería que hablaran con su hijo o hija para que esta situación no ocurra más. Gracias.

_____
(Firma del maestro/a)

- -

(Corten aquí y devuelvan esta parte a la escuela)

Penitencia

Les agradecería que firmaran este aviso y lo devolvieran a la escuela el próximo día escolar.

_____ Hemos leído este aviso.

_____ Queremos reunirnos con Ud. para hablar sobre este problema.

_____
(Firma del estudiante)

_____
(Firma de los padres)

_____
(Número de teléfono)

_____

Dear Family:

You are invited to visit our school for the following special event:

_____ open house

_____ special program

_____ musical program

_____ meeting for parents only

_____ PTA meeting

_____ PAC meeting

Date _____

Time _____

Place _____

_____ Child care will be provided.

_____ Child care will not be provided.

I hope to see you there!

_____
(teacher's signature)

_____

Estimada familia:

Les invito a venir a la escuela para la siguiente actividad:

_____ Noche para padres

_____ Programa especial

_____ Programa musical

_____ Reunión para padres (no niños)

_____ Reunión de la PTA

_____ Reunión de la PAC

Fecha:_____

Hora:_____

Lugar:_____

_____ Se ofrecerá cuidado de niños.

_____ No se ofrecerá cuidado de niños.

¡Espero verlos allí!

_____

(Firma del maestro/a)

_____

Dear Family:

I would like _____ to stay after school
(child's name)

on _____ until _____.
(date)   (time)

He or she needs to

_____ complete unfinished work

_____ work on a special project

_____ help in the classroom

_____ participate in a sport or physical education activity

Thank you for your cooperation.

_____
(teacher's signature)

- -
(Cut here and return to school.)

_____ has my permission
(child's name)

to stay after school on _____ .
(date)

_____
(parent's signature)

_____

Estimada familia:

Me gustaría que _____ se quedara en la escuela
(Nombre del estudiante)

después de las clases el día _____ hasta las _____.
(Fecha)   (Hora)

Él/Ella nesecita:

_____ Terminar su tarea.

_____ Trabajar en un proyecto especial.

_____ Ayudar en la clase.

_____ Participar en una actividad deportiva o de educación física.

Gracias por su cooperación.

_____
(Firma del maestro/a)

- -

(Corten aquí y devuelvan esta parte a la escuela)

_____tiene nuestro permiso para quedarse en
(Nombre del estudiante)

la escuela después de las clases el día _____.
(Fecha)

_____
(Firma de los padres)

_____

Dear Family:

Our class is having a special classroom activity

on _____ at _____.
             (date)   (time)

The activity is

_____ guest speaker or group

_____ class project

_____ class performance

Money needed?

No _____ Yes _____ Amount: $ _____

Parent help needed?

No _____ Yes _____

Please let me know if you will be available to help. Thank you.

_____
(teacher's signature)

- -

(Cut here and return to school.)

Yes, I will be able to help with this activity.

_____
(parent's signature)

_____
(telephone number)

_____

Estimada familia:

Nuestra clase va a tener una actividad especial

el día:_____ _____
                    (Fecha)   (Hora)

La actividad consiste en:

_____un orador o un grupo invitado

_____ un proyecto de la clase

_____ una representación de la clase

¿Se necesita dinero?

No _____ Sí_____ Cantidad: $_____

¿Se necesita ayuda de los padres?

No_____ Sí_____

Les agradecería que me dejaran saber si Uds. pueden ayudar.

_____
(Firma del maestro/a)

- -

(Corten aquí y devuelvan esta parte a la escuela)

_____ Sí, podemos ayudar con esta actividad.

_____
(Firma de los padres)

_____
(Número de teléfono)

_____

Dear Family:

There will be a field trip to _____
                                            (place)

on _____.
        (date)

Departure time: _____ Return time: _____

Transportation: _____ school bus

                _____ walking

                _____ private cars

Sack lunch: _____ Yes_____ No

Money: _____

School telephone:_____

_____
(teacher's signature)

- -

(Cut here and return to school.)

_____ has my permission to attend
    (child's name)

the field trip on _____.
                        (date)

_____
(parent's signature)

_____
(telephone number)

_____

Estimada familia:

Nuestra clase irá de excursión a _____
(Lugar)

el día _____.
(Fecha)

Hora de salida: _____ Hora de regreso: _____

Medio de transporte: _____ Autobús de la escuela

_____ Caminar

_____ Coches privados

Se necesita traer un almuerzo: _____ Sí _____ No

Dinero: _____

Número de teléfono de la escuela :_____

_____
(Firma del maestro/a)

- -

(Corten aquí y devuelvan esta parte a la escuela.)

Favor de llenar este aviso y devolverlo a la escuela.

_____tiene nuestro permiso (___ Sí ___ No)
(Nombre del estudiante)

para ir a la excursión el día _____.
(Fecha del viaje)

_____
(Firma de los padres)

_____
(Número de teléfono)

_____

Dear Family:

We will have a class party on _____.
(date)

_____ Please send $ _____ for treats.

_____ Please furnish a drink for _____ students.

_____ Please furnish a snack for _____ students.

If you have any questions,
please contact _____
(bilingual contact person)

at _____ .
(telephone number)

Thank you for your help.

_____
(teacher's signature)

_____

Estimada familia:

Nuestra clase tendrá una fiesta el día _____.
(Fecha)

_____ Favor de enviar $_____ para bocadillos.

_____ Favor de enviar una bebida (refresco, jugo)

para _____ estudiantes.

_____ Favor de enviar bocadillos para _____ estudiantes.

Si tienen preguntas,

pueden llamar a _____
(Persona bilingüe)

al _____.
(Número de teléfono)

Gracias por su cooperación.

_____
(Firma del maestro/a)

_____

Dear Family:

School pictures will be taken on _____.
(date)

These pictures may be purchased. Please see the attached price

sheet or call _____
(bilingual contact)

at _____ if you have questions.
(telephone number)

_____
(teacher's signature)

_____

Estimada familia:

Las fotos escolares se tomarán el día _____.
(Fecha)

Ustedes pueden comprar estas fotos. En la hoja adjunta
aparecen los precios.

Si tienen preguntas, pueden llamar a _____
(Contacto bilingüe)

al _____.
(Número de teléfono)

_____
(Firma del maestro/a)

_____

Dear Family:

Our school library is available to all students. Your child may check out books each week at the regular library day for our class or during free time when the library is open.

Reading books is an important part of the reading program in our school. Please set a time for your child to read books on a regular basis at home.

Books are usually borrowed for a period of _____ week(s). Please return the books when they are due or on our regular library day, _____.

It is important that the books are handled carefully and kept in a safe place at home. Please remind your child that it is his or her responsibility to care for the books. If a book is lost or damaged, please contact the school as soon as possible so that a replacement may be ordered.

Happy reading!

_____
(teacher's signature)

Estimada familia:

Todos los estudiantes pueden usar la biblioteca de nuestra escuela. Su hijo o hija puede sacar libros cada semana durante el día de biblioteca asignado para nuestra clase, o durante algún tiempo libre cuando está abierta la biblioteca.

La lectura de libros es una parte muy importante del programa de lectura de nuestra escuela. Es importante que ustedes separen una hora fija para que su hijo o hija lea en la casa todos los días.

Los libros se pueden sacar prestados regularmente por un período de _____ semana(s). Los libros se deben devolver en su fecha señalada, o en nuestro día asignado a la biblioteca, _____.
(Día de la semana)

Es importante cuidar los libros mientras que estén en su casa y guardarlos en un lugar seguro. Recuérdenle a su hijo o hija que es él o ella quien tiene la responsabilidad de cuidar los libros. Si el libro se pierde o se daña, les agradecemos que notifiquen este hecho a la escuela para que puedan reemplazarlo. ¡Qué se diviertan leyendo!

_____
(Firma del maestro/a)

_____

Dear Family:

_____ has the following library book(s) overdue.
(child's name)

Please help your child remember to return the book(s) as soon as possible.

Name of book(s)

_____

_____

_____

_____

Thank you for your help.

_____
(teacher's signature)

_____

Estimada familia:

_____ se ha retrasado en devolver los
(Nombre del estudiante)

siguientes libros a la biblioteca. Les agradecería que le recordaran a su
hijo o hija que debe devolver los libros lo más pronto posible.

Títulos de los libros:

_____

_____

_____

_____

Gracias por su ayuda.

_____
(Firma del maestro/a)

_____

Dear Family:

_____ has lost the following book(s).
        (child's name)

Name of book(s)   **Cost**

_____

_____

_____

If you are unable to locate the book(s), please send the money for replacement as soon as possible. Thank you.

_____
(teacher's signature)

- -

(Cut here and return to school.)

I am aware that _____ has lost a book or books.
                    (child's name)

_____ Book(s) returned.

_____ Money enclosed.

_____
(parent's signature)

_____

Estimada familia:

_____ha perdido los siguientes libros:
  (Nombre del estudiante)

Título del libro   **Precio**

_____

_____

_____

Si no logran encontrar los libros, les agradecemos que envíen el importe de los mismos lo más pronto posible para poder reemplazarlos.

_____
(Firma del maestro/a)

(Corten aquí y devuelvan esta parte a la escuela.)

Estamos al tanto de que _____ perdió
       (Nombre del estudiante)

un libro o varios libros.

_____ Libro(s) devuelto(s).

_____Importe por el libro(s) perdido(s).

_____
(Firma de los padres)